My Dark Garden

Poems and Meditations
For Life During and After
Diagnosis

by Mary Kathryn LeMaster

For the **part** of you that **thinks** you are alone, I have cleared a **seat**.

I **wrote** My Dark Garden to remember the power of my **voice.**

Planting **seeds** for wholeness after picking up **pieces** from diagnosis, becoming legally blind and learning how to **breathe** in the **dark**.

Connection

Ways to slow life down with me

Website:
www.themarykathryn.com
Instagram:
@themarykathryn_
Email:
breathebigmk@gmail.com

The recorded guided meditations from *My Dark Garden* can be found here:
www.themarykathryn.com
/my-dark-garden-downloads

Table of Contents

Seeds of My Story

My Dark Garden is about navigating the changing landscape that begins the day of diagnosis. The day I left the doctor's office, I felt like I had been handed someone else's title— one I never signed up for. By writing and sharing my lived experiences, I've taken back my power and strengthened my voice and purpose.

At thirteen, I was diagnosed with retinitis pigmentosa (RP), a rare degenerative eye condition that causes peripheral vision loss and, in some cases, total blindness. I was told I would be blind by my thirties—

a terrifying pill to swallow that reshaped my outlook for years. I was also deeply confused. At the time, I had so much vision that I couldn't imagine a future without it. Fear and loneliness lingered for a long time. But I was also a fiery teenager, determined that this diagnosis would not define me.

In the beginning, I lost my sight mainly at night. Over time, it crept into my peripheral vision during the day, leaving me with tunnel vision. I was diagnosed as legally blind much later, at forty-seven. That day I cried hard—but I also exhaled. I knew I was getting close, but I didn't know how much sight I had lost. I hadn't realized how long I had been unconsciously bracing for the day I would go blind.

What the doctors never told me is that blindness doesn't mean complete darkness—it's a spectrum.

Eighty-nine percent of the blind and visually impaired community still sees something: fragments of shapes, faces, colors, or even shades of light. Both of my diagnosis days were scary, confusing, and profoundly isolating.

Today, there is no cure for RP, and I

don't know if there will be one in my lifetime. What I do know is that I can —and I am—living a full, beautiful life with what I have.

After spending countless hours in doctors' offices over the years, hearing hard test results and predictions of how awful my life could become, I wanted to change the narrative: to hear my own opinion on how I wanted to live this new part of my life, to understand how it actually felt in my body, heart, and mind, and to ask: *What else was here for me? What was still possible—even in the dark?*

Currently, I have thirteen percent central vision, and I have become that woman who literally stops to smell every rose. My vision now extends far beyond what is physical.

Friend, if you don't already pause to experience the beauty around you, this is your invitation. You will never pass that bloom again. It is waiting for you to visit, to stand in awe, to take it in fully. My guess is it has a message for you—if you stay long enough.

Was this experience here to bring me closer to the true nature of who I am? A master gardener in the dark.

The greatest gifts I've given myself over these years are learning to slow down, to be with myself in the moment, to trust that I am the best expert on me, and to connect with community. Four decades of practicing and teaching meditation, breathwork, sound therapy, and energy frequency have carried me through the hardest days and reconnected me with my body and the intelligence of my senses.

I also know we are not meant to live in isolation. Creating and connecting with supportive communities—for myself and for others on a similar path—has been like a lavender balm for my soul.

Like the wide roots of trees, we support and hold one another. And when we are full, we can reach out to lift another toward the sun.

There will be days, living with a degenerative diagnosis, when grief grows like weeds.

And there will be other days, when the most beautiful blooms appear— blooms that exist only because of the weeds.

Both things can be true at once. The day of diagnosis shakes us open: to breathe, to connect with our bodies in new ways, and to hear the voice of our true spirit.

Nothing is broken; it just needs tending and care.

Before You Begin:

As you make your way through the poems in *My Dark Garden,* I hope you see yourself in them and feel us walking together. No matter your diagnosis, the layers of emotion are similar.

This collection moves through three stages of my diagnosis journey: **Uprooted, Clearing Ground** and **Watering Blooms**.

In each section, there are **Space to Breathe** pages, **Grounding Meditations,** and **Seeds** as gentle stops along the way.

Take your time moving through these, and tune in to what your body, heart, and mind need as you feel into your own diagnosed experience.

On the **Space to Breathe** pages, go for a walk, stretch your body, rest, or even dance.

For the audio version of the guided meditations, there is a link found in the **Connection** section prior to the Table of Contents. Get comfortable and grab your headphones for deeper relaxation.

UPROOTED

Dear Doctor

Can you see **me**?
My parents, great aunt and
cousins too.
You don't need a shovel or to **dilate**.
Cover your
right eye with your **left** hand
and say my name.
Eye **to** eye heart to **heart.**

Unbutton

Sit still and **quiet**.
We have to get
more **of** you
to tell you what's
wrong with you.
Sit back and **relax**.

Me

Hang on, let me see what I don't.
Move to the left.
Mine, not **yours**.
It still **doesn't** work.
Turn the clock back,
maybe my **vision** is there.
I **know** I dropped it along the way,
can you **help** me?

Space to Breathe

Slowly inhale
Softly exhale

Title

Thirteen lies were
glowing in the dark
and you didn't see **one**.
I **realized** they blinded
you half way through.
Put your **heart** in a jar and
walked away. Don't **worry**,
the dark and **lonely** will send
a map to help you **find** your way
back.
We will be **here.**

Aloe

I think the **nurse** is trying to
hand me a tissue,
but I **can't** see.
She kindly places
one in my hand
then wipes my eyes dry.
I am right **here**,
if you need me.

Blindness

The **silence**
you're offering is **not** for me.
I can **see** all that
you can't feel.
The **gifts** of a
blind mystic.

Seeds

If you could tell your doctor, family members, or friends how you really feel about your diagnosis, what would you say?

Soul Drops

I **can't** move yet,
my eyes are **still** adjusting.
It doesn't matter,
we **need** the room and
the world will not always
wait for you.
Have a seat in the **blue** chairs and
see **you** in six months.

How

Stay afraid and **you** will
lose your **ability** to erase every "no"
anyone has ever told you.
They will **tell** you,
you can no longer grow,
but pull that **weed** and plant
a **giant** oak of possibility.

Rose

Leaving with the new title
you gave me and
I **hate** it.
Everything **changed** so fast.
I want to push to the next
piece but **my** body knows
better. Feeling the tears run,
letting **them** fall.
I am here to **hold** you.

Hang On

I made **sure** no one
knew **there** was
pain for 37 years.
Say it's all fine,
laugh as I fall off the step,
clench my mouth shut,
smile through the lies.
Pretending was my
family's most **bountiful** crop.

Lies

Take **my** story
out of your mouth.
This vision is not for sale.
I **carved** my own key from
the fallen pecan a long time ago
that I knew you **would**
never see.

See

Excuse me,
you dropped your words
while not being able to
look me in the **eye**.
It's not over **was** all you
had to **say**.
Not one of **you** have told me
I also **will** have a beautiful life.
Can't you see?
The light is dying to **come** in.

Grounding Meditation:
Waiting Room Rx

Plug in your headphones, get comfy, and have a listen.

Take up space in your seat, and let yourself feel whatever you need to feel.

This is your experience—there are no rules for how to navigate it.

Inhale a little deeper. Feel your feet on the ground.

Exhale a little longer. Soften the space behind your heart, sit up tall, and feel the support in your legs.

What if the whole world is cheering you on right now, right here in this waiting room? What if everyone here is on your team?

What if the person next to you is feeling the same thing you are—that you are not alone?

Give yourself more options than what you've been handed. There is something bigger behind it.

What song do you want to hear right now? Breathe and press play.

CLEARING GROUND

Sense

What will I do
if the **lights** really go out?
I will die
and then **say** hello.

Moon Party

Combing the night sky
the stars **glimmer**,
but I can't find the moon.
My eyes closed and heard
the lunar whisper,
"My light was placed
inside your **bones** years ago
so you wouldn't
have to search **outside**
of your own skin.
Smile, bright girl,
we are **one**"

It's Mine

My **forehead** still bloody from
the corner of the cabinet
door I never **saw**.
My **old** friend pain reminding
me to move **slower**.

Windows Down

Let the license **fly**.
Hung my keys up five years ago
my eyes still fill with **sadness**.
I miss the conversations during
school pickup and drop off.
Don't **know** if this will ever go away.

Queen of Darkness

The **turquoise** floor
feels warm, my breath
smooth, feet **sturdy**.
Vision gone again **I've**
lost it. Where the **fuck**
is the door?
Start all over
Again

Tetons

Only a **sliver** of light
reflecting on the back
of **his** climbing boots.
Pitch black, harsh wind cutting
the air.
Don't quit **now**,
breathe, move your feet.
One **more** step, MK.
The gifts from the peak
are ready to **slip** into
the right chamber of your heart, the
place you thought **would** be empty
forever.

Space to Breathe

*Take the biggest
breath you've taken all
day and fully let it go*

Show Me

You and me **Sugar**,
let's hit it.
What's on deck?
A curb, a crowd, a display,
a wet floor sign
Roll **in**.

Shadows

I let shame **out** of the
window so I could
see and *feel* all of me.
Checking under its shadow
to see that **soil** of **light** had
lined the walls of my mouth and
down my throat.
Moonflowers glisten
on the chord of my voice.
Truth telling, way showing,
these grounds are
for healing.

I Know

Blindness is not a
death sentence,
It's the key to an **entire**
new world. **Sight** that
you have never felt before.

Seeds

*What permission do you
need to give yourself
to make this journey your own?*

Leftovers

You don't **look** blind.
Really?
I thought I **fit** the image.
Lens one is clear.

Home

I **will** always
find my way home.
I am **not** afraid.
There are no **patterns**
of shoulds here.
The **dark** has always
been my way **in**.

Hello

Bees cracked the door open for lightning bugs to fly across my line of **vision**.
Don't **forget** you are real.
See all of **you**.
Even the **part** that makes your palms sweat.
It's **also** magic.

Follow

I saw your **eyes**
in the **same** box and
they wept like mine.
Our souls can **break**
in the beginning
of **being** cleared.
Lean in.

Bathroom Crawl

My **hands** glide across
the hot pink **lines** in the hallway
painting at three AM.
Trusting the **feedback**
of my fingers as I slowly
count each step **forward**.
Three more and one to
the right.
New **maps** in the dark.

Garden

Purposefully not watering **seeds**
of hopelessness.
They **keep** sprouting on their own.
Green bright leaves breaking
through the top layer of soil.
Maybe they have a new story
to **tell** that I **can't** understand.
Not to keep me back,
but to feel all the way through.
Sunlight **spotting** new codes.
Follow the natural path.

Grounding Meditation:
Permission to Let Go

To take care of your wellness in the best way you can, a reprieve from fixing needs to occur. What if, for the next five minutes, there is nothing to fix? No agenda, no questions to answer, no pressure.

Place your left hand on your heart— feel the contact between the palm of your hand and the center of your chest.

Place your right hand on your stomach—notice the weight and warmth of the palms of your hands and pads of your fingers.

Let your breath come into your hands.

Stay and breathe for ten rounds.

This simple awareness reminds your brain and body that it is okay and safe to be present, that you are grounded and supported by your power and presence. Tune in to how you are really doing, what do you really need? Breathe in a little longer, breathe out a little slower.

Words to feel supported by:

I am here now.

I am grateful for the breath I am breathing.

Nothing to fix, no pressure, no agenda.

Just me with my amazing self.

WATERING BLOOMS

Yarrow

Discovery call
through **it** all.
Blooming in a way
they told me not to.

I Will Take It From Here

I could **hear** the unbuttoning of
my old jacket as I walked **my** arms
out of the sleeves.
Unpacking vulnerability,
I finally saw my new self
in the mirror.
I no longer have to **run**.

Blink

If **I** could explain the dark
then you **wouldn't** have
to find your own.
It's **not** mine to give,
but I will **be** waiting
with **blooming** dahlias
at the gate on the **south** side.

The Puzzle

The disabled are not
searching
in the way you are.
We've adjusted our crowns
made extra room **for**
unmanicured love.
Nothing to fill
Nothing to check
Eyes **open**
Lungs **light.**

Space to Breathe

Inhale to the count of three
Exhale to the count of three

The Clock

I unlock old
stories to unburden
my feet. Shoulders push open
the gates to grow my **intuition**.
Air fills my **right** lung and
vision opens in the left eye.
Breathing slowly is the color
of my soul's ink.

Disabled

A map of intuition
and **ancestral** seeds.
A kaleidoscope of lines in
my heart, laced **with** energy sound
codes. I was born with the keys **in**
my **hand**.

Basil

Making the appointment
with **palms** sweating.
Once a year is too often for
them **to** tell me to plan
for the **worst.**
I know the seeds of my body
are not to **be** feared, but celebrated
and **adored.**

It's Time

I never **thought** I was
meant for this.
Didn't know I was
part of the bigger
plan **until** the
unseen flowers called
my name.
I, too, have their power.

Seeds

*What possibilities do
you want to plant?*

Return

Thank you for being who you
were that **day,** thank you for
the role you **played**.
I wrote new permissions
and **tucked** them
into a giant flame.
No longer carrying what you
need me to be.
I have walked my own path to heal
myself in this garden.

Dahlia

I **bask** in your folds of support.
Knowing **it's** not just for me,
but for **the** soul of the collective.
Sun equally smiling on **each** petal
inspiring **us** to wake up and shine.

Sage

Oh beautiful **body**, eyes, heart,
lungs, I **thank you**.
You've been telling me a story
I **have** been afraid to hear
for a long **time**.
I know **you** are not working against
me, you are **pulling** me closer.
To listen without distortion or shame,
but only **love** and celebration.
See me this **lifetime**.

Grounding Meditation:
Know You Are Not Alone

You may feel like you are the only person in the world going through what you are, but I promise there are many others leaving doctors' offices today with a similar diagnosis—feeling the same thing. Everyone will take one step forward when the time is right and will figure out the best game plan for what they need. Your job now is to take care of yourself the best way you can. Let this body scan help you soften and ease the worry from each part of the body.

Softly exhale to the count of three, let your shoulders drop down away from your ears.

Inhale to the count of three, let the muscles of your stomach soften.

Exhale to the count of three, relax your low back.

Inhale to the count of three, feel rest in your knees.

Exhale to the count of three, find ease in your feet.

Let your whole body relax.

End of the Path

Thank you for joining me in *My Dark Garden*. I will continue to cheer us on and stay aligned with the highest version of our lives.

Be good to yourself,
take gorgeous care,
and plant more flowers!

Breathe deep.

Love,
Mary Kathryn "MK"

Beyond the Garden

I am a legally blind visionary on a mission to help the world breathe a bigger breath. I foster connection through sound healing, public speaking, guiding slow living practices, developing accessibility and mindfulness strategies, advocacy, and teaching others how to keep their peace—especially when life grows dark.

I live in Texas with my husband, our son, and our four-legged companions. I'm committed to sharing my journey and the power of healing through words, creativity, and joy.

My Dark Garden is my offering to all who seek a path to wholeness, however winding or shadowed it may be.

I teach empowering self-care practices both in-person and virtually. You can learn more about my work and offerings at www.themarykathryn.com

www.ingramcontent.com/pod-product-compliance
Lightning Source LLC
Chambersburg PA
CBHW030914140626
46545CB00017B/2352